MW01441298

Queen of Know

Conversations with Centenarian

Jule Moon

For Bill

Donna F. Orchard

Donna Orchard

An Intellect Publishing Book
Copyright 2024 Donna Orchard

First Edition: 2024
ISBN: 978-1-961485-36-5 Hardback
ISBN: 978-1-961485-49-5 paperback

FV-10

All rights reserved. No part of this book may be reproduced in any form or by any electronic, mechanical, or other means now known or hereafter invented, including photocopying or recording, or stored in any information storage or retrieval systems without the express written permission of the publisher, except for newspaper, magazine, or other reviewers who wish to quote brief passages in connection with a review.

Please respect Author's Rights.

Intellect Publishing, LLC
6581 County Road 32, Suite 1195
Point Clear, AL 36564
www.IntellectPublishing.com

Foreword

My Aunt Jule Moon has been a larger-than-life presence in my world for over five decades. I was only fourteen when she cemented her status as "Favorite Aunty" during a visit to our home in Lakewood, Colorado. She sat me down on the living room floor, her sitting cross-legged like a meditating Asian monk, me with my knees to my chin. Aunty was going to tell me my fortune with her tarot cards. No other kids I knew had an aunt that was that cool!

As I grew older, I began to understand her stories of growing up, getting married, changing careers from geologist to social worker, and the other interesting aspects of her life. She didn't visit us often in Colorado but was always staying in touch through handwritten letters that, even back then, were hard to read. Handwriting was not her strongest skill set, but she never missed sending us three kids a birthday card.

After Aunty moved to Fairhope in the late 90s, I visited her at her home. She introduced me to her childhood friend Mary, who lived across the street and was having an informal party the afternoon I arrived. It was impressive how they had stayed in touch through the years and were so close. Another high school friend, Helen was at that party and I could see theirs was a bond few of us have in our 80s. It was during that visit we drove to Mobile and she showed me the house she and my father lived in, her a teenager, my dad pre-teen. Seeing Mobile through her eyes was a treat and gave me entrance to their world. I even got to see her high school.

Sadly, her friend Mary died just a few years later, and it seemed each new year brought the passing of one of her friends.

Yet somehow, Aunty kept her head up and her attitude positive. Part of her joy in life was her sheltie dog, Laddie. Walking Laddie was good for her physical health and mental health. Laddie was an ambassador of goodwill in the neighborhood and was a source of pride and joy to Aunty.

When I started travel and food writing in 2015, Aunty was very supportive and helped me work out some challenges with grammar and spelling. I remember sending her one of my published articles, which she returned to me with her edits. I told her, "Aunt Jule, that story was edited by a professional magazine editor"! Aunty said, "Well, they missed a few things in that story that somebody should have caught." That was when she was around 98 years old and still very sharp. Aunty was still driving at 100 writing poetry, and cooking her own meals. She kept cooking but soon gave up driving after turning 100, much to my relief.

I became her Power of Attorney and Medical Power of Attorney by mutual consent about the time she turned 96. Through the challenges of losing her ability to take care of cooking, laundry, shopping, etc., she adjusted to the harsh realities of growing old. The hardest part of the move from her home was having to give up her new dog Buddy, but a dear friend provided a home for the pup and brings him to her for weekend visits. Giving up most of her antiques, art, and books was also a crushing blow, yet she handled that task gracefully.

Even though she is 104, we still talk by phone, usually 2-3 times each week, and I visit a couple of times per year when I can get away from my duties at home in Baltimore. She is an inspiration to me and my siblings on how to survive and thrive into advanced age. I hope you enjoy reading about her and gain inspiration on how to age gracefully and lead a good life. May we all find the priceless friendships that have helped her through the years.

Kurt Jacobson

Acknowledgements

The very definition of 'memoir' is that you look at a life then leave out much of it. Jule Moon is a loving friend who shares stories and wisdom with me from her multifaceted experience. There are no dull moments with Jule. I visit one or two times a week, not to cheer her up, but to sit at her knee and laugh or cry at her indefinable brilliance. She is now105. Who can try to be prepared to lose a friend you love at any age?

I also want to thank John Woods. He supported this idea from its inception. "Jule Moon, yes, he says." He knew, as I did, when you stop to chat with Jule, she relates customary stories in unimaginable detail. For about three years, I looked around my office crowded with stacks of papers, notes, Indian relics and even Jule's clothing. John finally says, "Send me a manuscript."

Thanks for everything to my longtime partner, Bill. He finds the patience to meet my day-to-day problems with technology. His consistent loving kindness underlies all of my work.

Donna Orchard

Queen of Know

Conversations with Centenarian
Jule Moon

Donna Orchard

Chapter 1

Recognition

Last night Jan left for the night as usual. Something bad happened, Donna. Come sit down. When I tried to get to the bathroom during the night, I could not twist around, scoot to the edge of the bed, and push up with my arms. I couldn't get out of bed! My muscles…my muscles gave up on me. I am helpless. Helpless! (Crying)

I am so sorry, Jule. Let me get a cool cloth for your head. It will be okay. You can call Kurt today and tell him what is happening. Keep the cloth on your head… Your skin is beautiful this morning, glowing in this pink gown.

My cheeks are always rosy.

Do you understand what this means? I will require around-the-clock care. Kurt says I don't have the money, says we will have to sell the house to get cash for that kind of care at home. I don't want to sell my house, Donna. It's the only thing I've got, the only thing I've got… (Crying)

All this stuff, I will never be able to organize it. It's just stuff to Kurt, but to me, it is my life. He's my favorite nephew, but he can't tell me what to do.

I've heard Kurt whisper to my friends that we should start thinking about a nursing home.

I won't go. I'd rather die. None of them will take Buddy. I'm not going anywhere without my dog. He needn't talk to me about a nursing home.

I'm so sorry, Jule. Nobody has said 'nursing home.' Don't worry about living there right now. You think about LIVING.

I have to worry about it. You know I don't have children, Donna. Kurt is in Baltimore. He takes care of all of my finances. I love him and trust him, but I'm not going to a nursing home. I'd rather die.

Where is that woman who tells me the key to happiness is 'to adapt?' You have had great challenges all your life: a geologist, paleontologist, social worker, psychologist, psychotherapist, and antique dealer. But your greatest accomplishment is gathering people around you at every stage of life, people who love you. You chose to look change in the eye. And you have done it all with Southern elegance and grace, My Lady.

Beige, beige, all the walls are beige in those places, bla, bla, bla, bla. The so called art on the halls are zig zag. Everybody is too busy to stop to fix it. The four walls, all you can see in those places. I'd rather die.

I won't go anywhere without Buddy.

Excuse the pun but you are like a dog with a bone when 'nursing home' is mentioned.

I kind of like beige… Caught you smiling…

They won't let me set up my collection of Indian dolls. Look up on the mantel at their skirts sashaying in apple red, green and orange. I got those in the 40s when I was in Santa Fe, going to school at the University of Texas. When tourists got off the buses, the Indians would give away these little handmade dolls, free. The whole collection is probably worth about $150.00 today.

They will take my jewelry right off me: my earrings, bracelets, and rings.

Who will take your jewelry? Don't go there, Jule.

I need to call Kurt to see how many more years I can live before the money runs out.

It's not about the money! You are more important than money. Lots of people love you. You have kept up with your old friends all your life.

They're all dead.

Well, how about your young friends, like me in my 70s?

See. Because we know more about how to take care of ourselves, we are living longer.

Third time you broke our agreement, not to talk about DYING.

I am this old because I eat right—period. No wheat. No sugar. You have to pay attention to what you are doing. People don't pay attention to what they are doing. You know I'm diabetic. I was one point into pre-diabetic. I stopped it right there. How do you think I lived to be over 100? I watch what I eat.

I also have many allergies. They wouldn't let me join up in WWII because of my allergies. I wanted to join up after Pearl Harbor. We all did. They needed me in the Pacific but the military couldn't send me there with asthma. Long lines to sign up.

I'm allergic to wheat, fruit, carrots, beef, catsup, fruit juices, and bread (unless it is gluten free), all cake, pie…

No cinnamon rolls? Now I'd rather die.

Every time I come in here you are eating lettuce with sparse colorful stuff mixed up in it.

My point. But I don't eat too many carrots. They have a lot of sugar in them. Once I start eating a carrot, I want to gobble up the whole thing.

What could be wrong with a carrot? It is a root grown by God. They are on my 'healthy' list. Do you know you can actually turn orange if you eat too many carrots? That's true.

Your mind is better than mine. You can tell me what you had for breakfast yesterday. You called out "Eric Holder" before I could think of it when we talked Obama politics. Remember?

Donna, why don't you eva wear pink?

Got to go. Love ya, Jule.

Chapter 2

A Fair Hope

One might predict Jule Moon's resolve to anchor herself to Fairhope, Alabama, in preparation for old age.

Fairhope, was founded in 1894 by a group of populist reformers from other states. They were looking for a utopia to establish a Single Tax Colony, a plan to raise all government revenue from a single tax on land values. One member remarked, "We have a 'fair hope' of succeeding."

Ernest Berry Gaston, a young Iowa journalist, established the model community on Mobile Bay, what he called "cooperative individualism."

Jule Jacobson was born in 1919, twenty-five years too late to stand with these founders. However, when I look over the edge of the bluff today, a romantic notion persists. Jule, this idealistic but practical young woman, joins with the parade of others at the communal bay front to begin their experiment.

The founders of Fairhope bring with them starry-eyed visionaries with imagination and tenacity, freethinking people: writers, actors, artists, and craftspeople. Today the town surrounds their colorful ancestors with beds of red, white, purple and yellow flowers on every corner, more horticulturalists than police officers.

Chapter 3

White Ermine Gown

I arrive early for my first visit to the Fairhope Unitarian Fellowship. Awkwardly, I take a comfortable armchair in the foyer and look out the large picture window. Someone finally approaches, deliberate and unhurried, an elderly woman. The cane goes down into the gravel, cane and step, cane and step. Happy to have something to do, I grab the door. She makes her entrance, tall and thin, monochromatic in cherry-blossom pink sequins. Below is the fluidity of a straight rose skirt to the ankles. The orange-red scarf is pinned in harmony around her neck with a burst of rhinestones. Her throwback to the 50's strikes me as elegant, fit for the symphony or maybe the theater in Mobile later in the day.

Can you help me with these bags?

She has never seen me. Nevertheless, I take the three gingham bags as she guides me into the kitchen; three bags, three hooks. I spot an organizer. Suddenly, a flashback to my clothes piled high in the closet, my best intention to put them on hangers—someday.

I hope we get along. I do like to preen in the pleasure of colors: strong aqua, burnt orange, and apple red. This woman is all pastels, no accident.

Soon I relax into her natural acceptance as she moves about quickly in the kitchen, a rhythm without wasted motion.

An educator, I know when to wait for instructions.

You can find the trays for cookies in that cabinet. Pull those 'store bought' cookies out of the bags. We hope to have homemade sweets, but we must always be prepared. What did you say your name was again?

Donna. Donna Orchard. Just like the apple orchard.

I'm Jule, J-u-l-e, pronounced 'Julie.' It was my mother's idea. Daddy wanted the traditional spelling. Mother could be amenable, but this time she was bullheaded. She didn't know she was foreshadowing my life as a poet. She told him "Jule' will look better when written." My father was 'Julius.' Sometimes people think I'm a man when they see my name. In Atlanta I was recognized for being editor of our prize-winning school newspaper, the *Murphy High News*. Mr. Jule Moon was put in the program. I'll never get over that!

How do you remember all these details?

I remember everything that has ever happened to me. I can recite the first poem I ever wrote for someone else. I was in third grade when our teacher asked us to write a poem about Christmas.

Um…Can I hear it?

> Christmas time is coming
> The snow is sifting down
> It lies about like a blanket
> Or a queen's white ermine gown

What is an ermine gown?

Ermine is a type of weasel with a white coat. Don't you know that?

I do now. Will you quote it again? I get a block when I find out you knew so much about weasels in third grade. I must have been asleep when we covered the weasel chapter.

***

Here, start with the ginger snaps. There is a proper way to open a bag of cookies so they don't crumble. Take these scissors. You have to pay attention to what you are doing, at all times. Most people don't pay attention to what they are doing.

I have a pretty good idea she is about to show me how to open a bag of cookies. I already know—*fast.*

Look, each cookie with like textures forms a brown spiral until they soar to the top in the middle of this large red platter, Donna, like this. Beautiful.

This is the poem I wrote today.

> I wish I liked your modern verse
> I wish you were not so perverse
> I wish you were not so dense
> Or it might make some sense

I think in stories and the story becomes a poem. A poem is about rhythm. Some of this stuff people write is not poetry!

How many poems have you written?

Oh, that's impossible. Listen to another poem I started today.

> Graduation
> Ending
> Chasing time
> Only two choices I could see
> Only one destined to be mine
> Only one befitting me

Which one did you choose?

It doesn't matter. You didn't understand the poem!

Ok.

You won the Pensters Writing Groups' poetry contest one month when I was sure I was going to win.

You are in Pensters Writing Group!? There are so many members. We have one hundred fifty on roll now... Oh, you sit on the front row, don't you? I remember you now.

That was just luck. I'm all narrative. I wrote that one poem about music I heard when I was in Europe.

And so it is. My close friendship with Jule Moon evolves organically from her poetry and her life stories close-at-hand. I meet her at the door and we put cookies out each Sunday. When she is ready to go, I carry the three well-worn bags to her special gravel parking spot to the right of the front door. She pats the top of her lumbering white Oldsmobile, not as a functionary, but as a dynamic old friend. She knows she will have to sell the car soon— give up her independence –even to drive the two blocks to the Fellowship.

Jule, I will pick you up. You have to stop driving. You are 100 years old!

***

I'd like to visit you in your home sometime. Let me guess, your house is filled with colors and textures like your clothing.

Oh, yes. I sold my house in Kentucky and was able to buy this one in Fairhope. I always knew I wanted to return here. I grew up in Mobile, but came here to my friend's beach house in Fairhope in the summer.

I have a comfortable home in Fairhope, lots of art. Come visit. The door is unlocked. Come on in, but don't let Buddy out. He's my new Border collie, black and white. I told them at the Haven Shelter, "I want a Border." They are herd dogs.

Finally got one. I've had Buddy about a week. He'll bark and climb up on the screen door when you knock. Haven't had time to train him, but he responds if you put your hand up and say, ' NO.'

My first Border collie was Laddie. They are smart animals, herd small sheep. He was one of several dogs at the pound in Kentucky. When I walked by, he was the only dog to stop and look right at me. Then he came over to the fence and licked my hand. He chose me. He's the smartest dog I've ever had.

One of those mysterious moments, maybe even a sacred moment.

No, Laddie was sharp and high-spirited. He came over and licked my fingers. He chose me. It was a coincidence.

You tell me a person cannot do everything themselves. They must be thankful.

Thankful to the people in your life, Donna. My life is filled with people. I have life-long friends from childhood… Oh, they are all gone now…

I see those tears.

I'll be in the kitchen at the counter. Just come in and call for me.

***

Donna Orchard

Homestead Village Retirement Community, Fairhope, Alabama

Arf, arf, arf,arf
Who is it?

It's Donna from the Fellowship.
Who?

I peer around the door and find Jule sitting on a high stool at the kitchen counter watching her small TV that fits nicely under the cabinets.

Donna. How good to see you! Come on in.
You didn't let Buddy out did you?

No. I pushed him back from the door. He won't bite me, will he?

He just wants to play. I haven't trained him yet. Borders are smart.

What'cha watching?

Oh, old cowboy movies: I watch them all day long.

When you are not writing poetry.

Daniel Boone, Fess Parker; The Lone Ranger, Clayton Moore; Wyatt Earp, Hugh O'Brian and the rest.

You must like men, Jule.

Oh, Donna... I was married once to a geology professor. That's a long story. Bill was the love of my life. We never married.

Why are you all dressed up?

I have a routine. This is just a housedress. I haven't put my makeup on yet! Hand me my makeup bag, will you? Don't come quite so early.

You look beautiful sitting there in your pink and blue print. Your cheeks are rosy. Lovely skin. Do you get up every day and put on earrings, bangle bracelets up to your elbows and rings on every finger?

My cheeks are always rosy.

Oh, I forgot. I have to use, what we used to call *rouge*. That's not what it's called anymore. What is the word?...

I love jewelry. I'll show you sometime what I've got stuffed in every drawer. I have studied gems. I'm a gemologist.

Oh, yes, you said your first degree was in geology at the University of Texas. That makes sense.

Diamonds, sapphires, and rubies; silver and gold are precious gems. Opals and garnets are semi-precious. I collect costume jewelry too.

Some of the finest gold and silver are in my safe deposit box. Stowe's Jewelry is selling some of my pieces for me. I may need the money someday.

How are your gadgets hanging on the wall: scissors, garlic press, screwdriver, two sizes of pliers?

They are on a magnetic strip, Silly.

Oh, what a great idea! I spend lots of time diving into messy drawers. Occasionally I find what I want.

People don't think about what they are doing, even the most familiar tasks. You must pay attention. For example, when you are looking for a garment in a closet, you must take one hanger at a time. People grab a whole bunch and never find anything.

I've never thought much about hangers.

You ought to.

Wow, I see a print from Picasso's Blue Period. It has a provenance on the back.

It is just a reproduction. I'll give it to you if I ever have to pack up.

Oh, thanks. But you could sell it. You don't need to give away your precious things.

I want you to have it, Donna.

Thank you, Jule.

Got to go, now.

See you soon. I love you, Jule...

Hum. No response.

Oh, before you go, will you hand me a pen from that wooden pencil holder over there? I want the one with the white end. **This one?** Not that one.

Ok. This one??? No. the one next to it.

Later, Jule.

Two weeks later.

Who you dressing up for Jule? The cowboys?

Oh, Donna.

Your skin looks beautiful today.

I have noticed over the last few weeks, you are losing weight. Can I get some ice cream or something for you? Can you eat ice cream? If I was heading for my 100th birthday, I'd have a hot fudge sundae every day with my cinnamon roll.

You wouldn't live that long!

The key to happiness is that you must adapt.

Yes, I have found one kind of ice cream I can eat. Go to Publix. It is called Pabin. Get me chocolate if they have it. I'm diabetic, you know, but I don't take the medicine. I control it with my food.

How do you spell that ice cream? I'll go by Publix.

P a b i n

A Week Later

Jule. I'm looking in the freezer. You haven't opened your ice cream! It cost me over $5.00 for one pint!

I will pay you for it. I have money.

No. I don't want money, Jule. That's not the point. I want you to eat.

Oh, I know it. I will. Thank you for getting that nice ice cream for me. I haven't gotten to it. You want some? Here why don't you take it home. Will your grandchildren eat it?

No! Wasn't it the right kind? I bought a pint of Chocolate Pabin made with skimmed milk. That's what you told me to get.

When did you begin a love/hate relationship with food, Jule? Are you anorexic?

No. I've never been anorexic.

Thank you. I'll get to the ice cream. I have so much food around here.

Food! I eat lots of fruit every day.

Has too much sugar. Fructose is still sugar.

What eyebrow pencil do you want me to pick up?

Oh, yes, that is Cody in 'fawn satin.' See what my eyebrows look like? That is the only color I use, only 'fawn satin.'

How did I know that?

I'll give you the money. I have money.

I know. What if I can't find 55 base. Would 54 do?

Oh, they have it. It's all at Walgreens. No, don't buy it if it is not 55. That's my color. Did you write it down?

Yes, Jule, I know you love Walgreens. They have everything to keep a person alive. You should do an ad for Walgreens.

Fifty-five, Amber Rose; I also need Elizabeth Taylor powder. It has a soft powder puff. I love it after my bath.

They won't have that! No one knows who Elizabeth Taylor is anymore. She died thirty or forty years ago.

They have it at Walgreens.

Yes, they did forty or fifty years ago!

What have you been up to?

Oh, I'm helping with your 100th birthday party! We are going to put a big 100 on the cake. I'm so excited. What color roses do you want on the cake?

I don't want a cake. I don't eat sugar.

What do you mean, you don't want cake? Hum. Hum. Well, we have to write on something, Jule. There will probably be sixty or seventy people at the Fellowship that day to celebrate your special birthday. Your nephew, Kurt, from Baltimore, and others will be here.

Sure, go ahead and get a cake for the rest of them. I won't eat it.

I won't eat cake. Others will enjoy it.

Oh, you can eat a small piece of birthday cake once a year!

You know I'm diabetic! I was one point into pre-diabetic. I stopped it right there. How do you think I lived to be 100?

Can't argue with that.

I never see you eating anything but lettuce with cucumbers, peppers, or onions mixed up in it. If it's lunch, you are having a lunch salad. Dinner? A dinner salad. I think you are too thin.

What can a person do when their body gives up before their mind?

I didn't mean to make you sad. I'm going to tell all your friends to come to your birthday party.

They are dead. All of them. All gone.

I see those tears.

You have to think about what you are doing. Always slow down and think about what you are doing.

What I'm doing right now is planning your 100th birthday party at the Fellowship. You are not cooperating.

Pink.

Chapter 4

Coca Cola

Where were you born, Jule?

I have lots of bad luck because I was born in Atlanta on *Friday the 13th* in 1919.

I'm not superstitious. However, I'd say anyone who reaches their 100th birthday is lucky in life. Wouldn't you? That file of yours is extensive and the recall is just; not normal, very out of the ordinary, even amazing.

My bad luck begins before I am born.

Daddy knows the pharmacist, Joseph Jacobs, at Jacob's Drug and Soda Shop where he goes for coffee every morning. One day, Jacob boasts about a new syrup that Dr. John Pemberton discovers as a tonic for common ailments. It contains the Kola nut that holds caffeine and cocaine, an extract from the Kola leaf. Cocaine is legal at the time, used for medicinal purposes.

Mr. Jacobs asks my daddy if he wants to invest in this new drink. He says, "No, I'm a paper mill guy." Obviously, we would have been fabulously wealthy if my father had taken him up on it! He was offered a franchise three times.

Oh, yeah, I almost die when I am young.

I look at you now and know sure-enough, you must have dodged lots of bullets — and with pizazz. You had breast cancer when you were in your 90s?

I went ahead and got both of my breasts removed.

That is the second time I almost died.

When I am six years old, I'm confined to my bed for many months. It begins with the measles that develops into two kinds of bronchitis, then pneumonia. I cannot move for over six months. All I can do is lie in bed and read or write. Mother rushes into my room with a handful of books every morning: Snow White, The Bobbsey Twins, Aesop's Fables, Mother Goose…morality stories. I miss most of the first grade.

I listen as your memories go back many times to this one childhood experience. You seem to savor it as a transformational encounter; when wisdom is created for you and received for a lifetime.

Yes. As a child, adults surround me. I am the oldest with two younger brothers. My illness makes me independent, an observer of behavior and interactions. Writing a daily journal becomes a fixed practice.

Poems come to me often. I consider myself a poet. The log of what happens to me each day often becomes a poem or I get a poem from my dreams, just something playful. I am inspired to write a longer piece, an essay, occasionally.

***

I am a teenager when I write to Franklin Roosevelt a letter congratulating him when he was elected President in 1933. He writes me back!

Looks like your luck is changing.

Not so fast. My mother sends the letter to my aunt to brag on me and I never get it back. That is my mother. She wants the family to know I am a big success. I wish I still had that letter signed by Roosevelt. She should not have sent it to my aunt. She didn't even ask me!

Another good luck moment is when you see Clark Gable in the basement of that department store in Atlanta. Remember that story?

Yes, I just stand back and do not scream and crowd him like the other girls. Clark Gable looks at me way in the back and winks at me.

I know you are going to tell me which department store. Oh, Jule.

***

I was born in 1919 in the middle of the Spanish Flu Epidemic of 1918. There is a lack of vaccines for young adults. Mother tells me there are signs on some of the houses, the front or back, to tell people, 'This is a flu house.'

There is a second and third wave of the Pandemic of 1918, like what happened to us recently with Covid 19 in America.

Overcrowding in foxholes spread the flu. Then soldiers are packed into boats, returning from the war. The third wave happens during celebrations when the troops come home.

Between 1919 and 1932, the life expectancy fell seven years, 36.6 for men and 42 for women.

At the end of the Influenza Pandemic of 1918, 675,000 people were dead.

The Covid Pandemic of 2019 is estimated to have killed one million Americans so far.

Other important markers from 1919: the Treaty of Versailles officially ending WWI , Woodrow Wilson is President, European women earn the

right to vote and the White Socks throw the World Series to the Cincinnati Reds (who never thought the game was rigged).

The Red Stockings were one of the first teams to begin the 7th inning stretch, standing and swaying to sing, Take Me Out to the Ballgame, still a favorite today.

Take me out to the ball game,
Take me out with the crowd;
Buy me some peanuts and Cracker Jacks,
I don't care if I never get back.
Let me root, root, root for the home team,
If they don't win, it's a shame.
For it's one, two, three strikes, you're out,
At the old ball game.

***

So, you were a child in Atlanta during the "Roaring 20s"?

Yes. Children are promoted in those days. We put on shows, dancing and singing.

Children are very important. I take drama, elocution, and voice. We sing on the downtown stage in Atlanta.

Charles Buddy Rogers owns a nightclub in Atlanta. He married Mary Pickford when I was eleven.

You remember your age?

I also remember going to see Lindbergh in Atlanta after he makes his first nonstop flight to Paris.

We live on Linwood Street in a brick bungalow and have chickens in the backyard.

One Sunday, they cook my favorite little red hen. I am very angry, "Mother, you didn't have to kill my little red hen!"

Mother is often in the kitchen, a good cook. We have a housekeeper to clean the dishes and the house. Mother makes my clothes when I am a little girl. Mary Toulmin, my best friend, wears a blue jumper to school one day. I go home and tell mother, I want one just like hers. She says, "Okay, but yours will have to be a different color. Don't be a sheep."

***

Some children come to school in dirty or torn clothes during the Great Depression about 1929.

The Depression did not affect us as much as others because Daddy had a good job at the paper mill.

Of course, everyone is sad during these times and have to 'tighten their belts.'

I was ten years old when Daddy took me to my first funeral. I had never seen everybody dressed in black. A man had jumped out of a window and killed himself. That is how many of the hopeless people committed suicide during the Great Depression. I don't know what my Daddy was thinking when he took me to that funeral!

You must have been scared.

No. My daddy was with me. But I was too young to be taken to that funeral!

***

When I am older, mother takes me to Davidson-Paxton Department store in downtown Atlanta to pick out one good dress. When I am about thirteen, she decides it is time to let me take the bus and go shopping by myself. She hands me bus fare and four dollars. I came home after finding a sale and hold up four dresses. Mother scolds me and tells me she wanted me to buy one 'good' dress.

When you chose gloves at this fancy department store, you were seated at a counter for the right accessory "to go with your clutch."

My mother likes elegant clothing, but no jewelry, very plain. When she buys a new dress, she pulls off the brooch attached and asks me if I want it. Of course, I do. It is costume jewelry, maybe a rhinestone encircled with stones. I've always loved jewelry. As you can see I have drawers full of it, all kinds.

After 1925, Davidson-Paxton's downtown store moved to Peachtree and Ellis. In 1985, it became Macy's.

***

Were you close to your grandparents?

Mother's father lived with us. He was German, very strict and had a bad temper. I did learn some German.

He was thoughtful, however, and built a dollhouse for me in Atlanta. It was my little playhouse detached from the big house. My daddy got mad because grandfather spent so much money for a tiny house for me to play in. It had a separate roof, tiles in the bath—everything just like a real house. I turned it into a library and pretended to check out books.

***

I was very close to my grandparents, my father's parents. They were persistent influences in my life. In fact, when my mother got too ill to take care of my sister, brother and me, we were put in my grandfather's Studebaker in Cincinnati in the middle of the night. Daddy, our Big Papa and Uncle Gene took us to a small town in Louisiana to live. We are raised by this big close family. My first memory at three is when I follow my grandmother around in the kitchen and pull on her apron. I saw how my grandmother loved God and loved other people. I got that love from her.

***

I read the words in II Corinthians, a tribute from a daughter-in-law to her mother-in-law. That touched me.

I didn't know my paternal grandfather. He was a musician, a violinist, who came over from Germany. They gave him a job in a feed store in America. Can you imagine that? He was so miserable he went back to Europe to make a living as a musician. I saw him just once when he came to visit.

My father grew up in a "state of the art" orphan's home. His mother died when he was small. The two girls went to live with relatives, the two boys went to this orphan's home. They made sure that my father got an education.

We were Reformed Jews from Germany. Daddy took me with him to the Temple on Fridays and we read from the Torah out of his case.

***

I went by myself on a train to visit my aunt in South Carolina when I was about twelve. I was so excited. Daddy gave the Pullman Porter a tip to watch after me. I had a sleeping car.

***

The Pullman Porters were the first African American men after slavery who were able to travel across America. They came back and gave their neighbors a taste of what the rest of the country was like. Their stories helped start the big migration of Blacks to the large cities in the North. Porters were good role models, highly trained, and immaculately dressed.

Phillip Randolph Pullman hired only black men to be porters. But, guess what? All of the porters were called 'George.'

That was disrespectful!

I remember looking out of the train windows for miles and miles, just riding and looking. Then suddenly, somewhere in South Georgia, I stand up to get a better look. I can't believe my eyes. A house is on fire! In a large field, a two story wood frame house is engulfed in big flames. I see no people. I sit and think about those people for a long time. I wonder if they got out. If they did, they will have no place to live.

*****

My first memory is in Atlanta, sitting on the front porch in a swing, eating Post Toasties.

If I had to sum up my life in one word, I would say 'people.'

When I am about three, I slide off the porch with my Felix the Cat doll in my arms and go to visit the neighbors. In those days you have to turn a bell at the front door. I remember that I had to jump up to reach the bell.

Did your parents know where you were? Of course, it was safe in those days. Were the neighbors glad to see you?

Oh, yes. They all know me and invite me in. They talk to me or maybe offer me a cookie.

Chapter 5

Cocopilli

I brought some flowers from my yard, Jule, gingers. Have you ever seen this color? I thought all gingers were white. I bought these plants and they turned out to be this kaolin, white with a clear pink quality. The stamens are a darker pink.

I didn't know this was a ginger. Thank you, Donna. They are lovely, so unusual.

Aren't they romantic? I can bring more. They flower until August.

Turn them around. The green leaves should be in the back.

Ok. How is that?

No. Turn them all the way 'round. The leaves go all the way in the back.

They ARE in the back.

I can't see the faces on TV. Turn them around a little more away from the TV.

OK. How is that? Jule, I am not turning flowers again. (*She smiles.*)

I'm ready for hurricane Zeta with two bags of ice and two cans of beans.

Good.

A note of thankfulness always follows, even to people she sees often ---especially to friends she sees often:

Dear Donna,

The beautiful gingers greeted my Fairhope Writer's Group last night. I enjoyed your visit so much. It made me forget for a while how much I'm missing out on.

I'm trying to survive these last days before the election. I'm depending on Carville's mantra 'It's the Pandemic, Stupid!' What grieves me so much is the country's stupid citizens—all. It is about education or the lack of it.

I learned more in high school civics class than the majority of people voting for The Crazy Man.

Dear Fairhope Writing Group,

I want to thank you for your surprise Christmas gifts of satsumas, assorted nuts and the festive potholders you brought. I appreciate it and will make use of them. I feel blessed to have such thoughtful friends.

Our new anthology turned out beautifully, the cover. everything! Thank you for including my six poems. Will we sell the books again at Page and Palette?

Merry Christmas and love, Jule

Jule, I read about the qualities of someone who lives to be 100 and more, want to hear it?

Sure.

Along with parental longevity, those who live a long life are often adaptable to change, resilient, educated, and have decision-making skills. They want a habitual schedule and desire a sense of purpose. There is a need to control their usual routine and may be seen as stubborn. Many are habitual, organized.

Speaking of being "organized" we need to look in all of these boxes of clothes to see what you want to keep. We didn't know your house would sell in two days. Kurt has found a temporary—I mean a house on Gayfer— with a fenced in yard for Buddy.

I will need the money. I don't mind living in a smaller house. I know I need to get rid of some of these clothes. It's just so hard…

It will be fun, a giant sale out if your garage!

Okay, This looks interesting. What symbols are on this jacket?

I want you to have it, Donna.

I can't take this 'one of a kind' jacket. Don't you know you could sell it? It must be one of your American Indian treasures.

Those are your colors, black and caramel. Do you know who is on the back? Can you see it now? It's Cocopilli: the flute player. Don't you know that? The Choctaw reverenced animals: This is a cow on the pocket, then a pig, and goat on the other side.

Those figures don't look much like animals. I'm glad you explained the meaning. Thank you. How does it look?

I twirl around in the jacket.

I told you it was perfect for you.

A Few Days Later

Jule, let me tell you what happened the first time I wore my jacket. A young boy carrying my groceries to the car asked me why I had a picture of the devil on my jacket!

People don't know anything. It's sad. People don't even know how we treated the Indians. Did you tell him Cocopilli? Cocopilli?

Well. No, I didn't. I should have, but he didn't seem too interested in Native American history. I didn't know who Cocopilli was until…

People are ignorant if they don't read! Look at my closet. People don't pay attention to what they are doing. Some people grab a bunch of hangers wildly looking for something. They don't find it. If you want to find something in a closet, move one hanger at a time.

Queen of Know

I've already taken notes on your hanger lecture, Jule.

People don't do right. I tell them and they don't listen.

They won't hang up anything. They don't listen to what I tell them.

Jule must be channeling me in my closet. I yell and curse, swear something is missing, until I grab the right bunch. I'm usually missing my black silk Elaine Fisher camisole hiding from me under something that is under something else on the same hanger.

Okay, Jule, here are three sequin tops in this box: blue, pink and gray. I don't think you will have that many 'dress up' events.

I'm going to keep them all. I wore the pink one for my interview in the Mrs. Senior Contest when I was 86. I was the oldest contestant. What was your talent? I sang, but the sound went out in the middle of my performance. I didn't win. I wore this silver one to my 100th birthday party…

I got it. I got it, Jule. Ok. All the sequins go in the 'Don't Sell' box.

Hum, hum…May be seen as stubborn…

Chapter 6

On a Lake in the Moonlight

Did I ever tell you about the Campfire Girls?

Campfire Girls? Is that like the Girl Scouts?

More focused.

In third and fourth grades, for eight weeks each summer, I went to Campfire Girls. I became obsessed with the Southwest and the American Indian.

For those two summers, we are Native Americans, Cherokees in their country. Our Cherokee names are on our headbands, in colored beads. That's what we call each other. My name is Katawah that means earth, mountains and sky.

You can still remember your name?

Of course!

Early in the day, we pray to the wind and to the gods, and then set about certain things.

We have jobs: to gather leaves and wood, make fires, practice archery, shoot guns. I am an excellent marksman. I am a very good shot. I am not good at archery.

Beads are presented to us at the end of each day for what we accomplish. We sew them on our ceremonial gowns. They resemble the shells Cherokee women sew on their coats.

At night, we get into canoes and ride out on the lake in the moonlight like the Indians.

Let me guess, Jule, your ceremonial gown was covered with beads by the time you leave Campfire Girls.

Oh, yes! I felt like a Cherokee.

Your love for the Southwest and your interest in everything American Indian is all around your home: art, clothing, silver jewelry, and even this beautiful red wool blanket on your bed.

That was the long answer about how I chose the University of Texas after high school.

Also, I followed one of my mother's wise sayings, "Don't be a sheep." Most of my friends went to Auburn or to Tuscaloosa.

I have a story. Guess what happened one day? After I am grown, driving through Kentucky, I see a sign to the next town, Katawah.

I must say, it sounds like a spiritual moment, the name crossing your path.

No, it was just by accident, a coincidence. I didn't go to the town, but I knew the name was a real, a Cherokee name, not something made up.

Unpacking boxes to move house.

Do you think that your Camp Fire Girl experience at a young age inter- mingled with your curiosity about everything Southwest and the American Indian?

Oh, yes. Native Americans wear lots of jewelry. I find the tribal silver fascinating. They put lovely Indian blankets on the sidewalks and sell jewelry everywhere. Look at this long ring. It covers my whole knuckle. I never take it off. The businesswoman in me kicks in and I realize that someday the originals will be sought after. I had an antique shop in Fairhope and sold Indian jewelry later in life.

I learned everything I could about Native Americans.

Of course you did.

I am in Texas in the late 30s through the 40s. I watch women make sculptures without a kiln, with their hands. I call them sculptures. They call them pots. The large ones they carry on their heads filled with water or vegetables from a market.

My arm is naked. I can't find any of my silver bangle bracelets. I wore four on my right arm. I want a thick silver bracelet on this arm. I don't feel dressed.

I'm leaving for vacation, Jule. I'll mark on the calendar when I'll return.

Leslie Ann will check on you.

Two Weeks Later

I have a present for you from Ashville. For me? Oh, you shouldn't have!

Unwraps it slowly. Oh, just what I wanted.

I know it is not the perfect bracelet, the one she would have chosen for herself. It was silver (plate), turquoise (fake).

Did you see some turquoise?

Yes. On this tiny string on the bracelet is the name of the maker, Coventry. I can't make out the first name.

Oh, that's Sarah Coventry. She is the first designer to begin making Native American jewelry affordable. Look at this metalwork. It is beautiful. My arms are so tiny, everything falls off.

That's why I got this one. You can squeeze it to fit your arm. I want you to wear it!

Oh, I'll wear it.

What a relief.

Who would know you could give me "Sarah" Coventry, the bracelet maker? How can I be surprised that you can not only recall her first name but also give me her background? Oh, Jule.

On my next visit.

"Donna take this bracelet and keep it for me. It slides on my arm and bruises me. Look here. I can't wear it."

"Oh, I squeezed it on your tiny arm very carefully so it wouldn't do that. Are you sure the bracelet made that bruise?"

Geeze, she is impossible to please!

Photographs

Donna Orchard

Jule Marion Jacobson (In back)
left: Jay Lee Jacobson
right: Frank Norman Jacobson

Donna Orchard

Jule's Grandmother - Anne Wolfe Jacobson

Jule Marion Jacobson

Queen of Know

Jule with brother Frank Jacobson

*Jule's Parents: Julius Jacobson and
Lillian Levin Jacobson*

Donna Orchard

Favorite Border collie, Laddie

Jule and Willie Bean the honorary mayor of Fairhope

Donna Orchard

Bill Stephens and Jule in Kentucky

Jule was a charter member of the Fairhope Newcomers' Club (Originally the Welcome Wagon)

At her desk when she was a psychotherapist working with Dr. Speakman

Donna Orchard

Ready for Mardi Gras

*At a stylish "hat"
party in Fairhope*

Donna Orchard

The family home at 6 Bienville
in Mobile. Jule with her nephew
Kurt Jacobson

Jule and her brother

Donna Orchard

Julius Jacobson, her father

Sign over Jule's Antique shop in Fairhope.

Seminole dolls from Florida

Donna Orchard

Pots from an Albuquerque vacation when Jule was at the University of Texas

American Indian Cocopilli jacket (Cow on front)

Queen of Know

Rainbow Dancer: Zoonie Tribe

Donna Orchard

Chapter 7

You Probably Won't Work

I am twelve and the new kid on the block when we move from Atlanta to Mobile with an unfamiliar Jewish religion. The children accept me wholeheartedly and become some of my lifelong companions: Lathale Capland, Mary Morgan Duggan. Mary Toulmin, and George Widney.

My take away from *Sherds*, your memoir, is the rare love and connection you maintained with these childhood friends. They remained your devoted confidants.

You think you do everything alone. Oh, no—

You remind me often.

The seventh grade in Mobile is at Barton Academy, in a beautiful historic building in the center of the city. It was the first public school building in Alabama.

I know. They have begun to use it again after an extensive restoration. It's an International Magnet School now. Students must apply.

We buy a house in Mobile from Mr. Friend the president of I.P at 6 Bienville Street. It is a beautiful two-story stucco. My room was upstairs. The house is still there.

***

One day I see a little girl I didn't know playing down our street. When I go up to her to say 'hello' she says "I can't play with you because you killed Jesus."

Oh, no! Did you cry? That's so mean. Why did she say that?

Upset, I run back home to ask Daddy what she meant. He explains it to me and tells me I killed no one. It is my first recognition that some people may not like us because of our religion. Nothing like that has happened to me since.

***

High school is lots of fun at Murphy. It is an exceptional high school for a classical education: Latin, French, glee club, band, and drama.

When a senior, I am editor of the school newspaper. Seven of us on the staff are invited to the Conference of High School Journalists in New York City. We are on the train for three days going North. We finally get to our rooms in Greenwich Village. The best people in journalism are at the conference to greet us as we tour the New York Herald Office. I get an interview with Eleanor Roosevelt.

Oh, I remember one of her quotes. She was one of the first feminist!

She said something like, "Remember always that you have not only the right to be an individual, you have an obligation to be one. You cannot make any contribution in life unless you do this."

I must say, your great attraction is that you never hesitate to be an individual, Jule (even if we want to scream at each other at times.) I love that about you.

During that period, I also go to the 1933 World's Fair in Chicago with friends. I remember we see one of the very first TVs. It is small and you can't see much on it.

***

When Hitler becomes chancellor in 1933, my father says, "This is a sad day for the World." Of course, we are Jewish.

***

After I graduate from high school, my father is very smart: "You probably won't have to work, but you will need to get your education."

Neither of my parents went to college.

I see my mother succeed in her familial role while maintaining her independence, pursuing interests of her choice. I expect to do the same. Mother is an example of living a long, productive life. At eighty-nine she still plays bridge. She is an expert bridge player who competed in tournaments. In her 80s and 90s she starts watching bowling. She lived to be 101. I thought I would die that year when I reached 101.

Mother dresses in nice classical clothing but plain, no jewelry.

That always bothered you. Didn't it? What would she think of you now in your bangle bracelets and your pink drop earrings?

I become interested in stones from my mother. She does not wear any adornments. I always want her to. When a shiny pin comes on a new dress, she just throws it away or gives it to me. One day I say, "What are you going to do with this ring in your jewelry box?" Mother says, "Do you want it? You can play with it. It's a rhinestone from Woolworth's."

"Can I have it?"

"Oh, yes."

This little six-year-old girl thinks it is the most sparkling ring she has ever seen.

I pin a camellia on her for father's funeral and she pulls it off.

***

After high school Daddy says, "You have to go to a university below the Mason-Dixon Line." I visit three of the top Universities: The University of Texas, Duke, and The University of South Carolina.

"I will pay for your tuition and give you $30 allowance each month."

I must tell my grandchildren about this allowance! One is at Auburn and the other at Tuscaloosa.

I choose the University of Texas where there are 10,000 students. (Don't be a Sheep.) I'll have to adjust to a bigger place. I can't wait to get to college. I want to know everything! I am <u>intoxicated</u> by the idea of learning. High-strung and mercurial, when I get to there, I have to declare a major. I am energized by both the arts and sciences from high school.

There is geology, French , Greek (I had Latin at Murphy), English, psychology, civics. I decide to get a Liberal Arts Degree for a good foundation. Then I will decide what to do in graduate school. My advisor raises an eyebrow when I choose a double major in geology and literature.

Literature and writing is a challenge. I am surprised because I consider myself an accomplished writer from my experience with the Murphy newspaper.

I make a 'B' on my first English paper.(I think I should have an 'A, 'of course). On my second paper, I make a 'B+.' The title of my third essay is, "How to Make an 'A' on an English Theme." I make an 'A!'

I go in and sit way in the back, behind hundreds of boys, in my first geology class. The professor calls me up to the second row to sit with the one other girl.

Geology is simply the study of the Earth, all the rocks of the Earth. I have to memorize all of the minerals. I remember sitting in the bathtub saying all of them. This study led to my interest in gemstones and jewelry.

One time I found a garnet in the shape of a heart at an antique shop for five dollars in the 1950s. I knew it was rare so I bought it for my niece. I told her, "Be careful with it." She went swimming and lost the ring. She called me and asked me to get her another one!

***

I get in the liberal arts program and earn enough credits for degrees in geology, literature, and psychology.

When I come home on weekends from the University, we huddle around and 'watch' the radio to see what Hitler is doing. When he invades Poland in 1939, the U.S. begins to see the gravity of the situation in Europe.

***

Oh, I didn't realize we got into the war just as you were graduating from college.

Yes, after Pearl Harbor, everyone gets in line to sign up. Both my brothers are pilots, one a paratrooper and the other a fighter pilot. I am turned down for the Waves because of my allergies. They want someone in the Pacific. Obviously, I can't go there with asthma. I think I told you that. The Red Cross needs me in a hospital. That's where I serve.

World War II was an important influence in my life—a nation of different people came together for a common cause. Both my brothers made it home.

***

After the war, I go back to the University of Texas for graduate study. I become interested in paleontology, the study of fossils, a subset of geology. I teach paleontology for two years as a student assistant. Then I discover, I am no good at drawing. You have to be an expert in sketching to be a paleontologist. I don't finish my PhD.

Being a teacher changed the trajectory of your life, didn't it?

Oh, yes. When I am teaching as a graduate assistant, most of my students are soldiers coming home from WWII: captains, sergeants, privates. The G.I. Bill enables them to go to school.

Many come to Texas to find oil, the Texas oil they hear about in the fox holes.

I memorize their names on the very first day. That's what a good teacher does.

When the students find out we will be finding fossils—no oil— they are hostile and resistant. Many of them are having trouble adjusting to life at home. I see I need to calm them down. It is not a term then, but they are suffering from PTSD, Post-Traumatic Stress Syndrome. From that experience, I know I want to work with people. I am able to help the soldiers adjust to home and to achieve success in the class.

I go back to the University of Texas to get another Master's Degree, this time to become family psychotherapist. This takes me to California to study family dynamics and psychiatry.

Why do you have to travel to California to learn about family therapy? What year is it?

In the 1960s I come to believe *when one member of the family is in therapy, it has a dramatic impact on the family overall.* Up until this time, therapy is mostly individual. I want to work one-on-one with the men who return from the war and their families.

Do you know about Virginia? Let's see. She is famous. Wrote about the mind.

Oh, Virginia Satire. Is that right?

Yes. I travel all over the country to attend her conferences.

I read some of her books when I am losing my mind trying to teach big children, high schoolers. They think they are grown. It helps me to call them *children* in my mind.

My first job after I get my MSW is in a large state psychiatric hospital.

Someone there is lost—lost in the system. He has been a CEO of a company in Austin. Under stress, he becomes depressed and irrational.

I try to be open and listen to patients when they want to be discharged. I talk to Jean Comer, the social worker, and tell her, "In my opinion, Rick is not insane." She tells me to be nice with him, but be firm.

I check Rick's records and find a cousin who is a counselor in Mexico. I work it out with the hospital for this cousin to come get him. He drives up in a limousine.

Rick had gone from a large, fine house in Austin to five years in a psychiatric hospital. He was seventy-one years old when he got out.

In the next hospital, I am a supervisor and able to use unconventional therapies. For example, I discovered that roleplaying is useful in working with some psychiatric patients. They will often do better when they pretend to be someone else. We do plays for the other patients. It is lots of fun for them and for me.

When I teach, if I'm not having fun, I stop. We do something else. I never told my principals the main objective in my lesson plan was for us to enjoy ourselves.

Then I become a principal, I notice if the kids are having fun and interacting with their teacher. It goes back to Eleanor Roosevelt's declaration "Be an individual."

Wish I could stay, Jule. I must leave the Empress to rein over her empire in 167 B.

Chapter 8

Fortuneteller

What is the most wonderful thing that has ever happened to you?

I became a real fortuneteller.

I wasn't expecting that!

When I was about 16, my friends and I were bored on a Saturday night. We decided to go from Mobile to Pritchard to see what was going on over there.

We ran into a fortuneteller that night. We were a little afraid to go in. She looked like the ones on TV, with a colorful scarf around her head and a crystal ball in front of her. We stuck together. She held a deck of regular playing cards then asked us to pick one. "What card am I holding? "I said 7." She turned the 7 around and said, "You will be a fortuneteller."

Are you serious? What about when you became a geologist, a paleontologist, a psychoanalyst, or a psychiatric social worker? Those all rely on science.

"Wait until you hear."

The fortuneteller told my friend that she sees her in the water and it has influenced her life. This friend had fallen in water and her hearing was impaired for life.

I didn't think much about this encounter it until I got to the University of Texas. I ran into this same woman who was now a professor of parapsychology!

She asked me "Did you do it?" I told her, "no." She said she could send me to a woman who could train me to be a fortuneteller the same way she was trained—with cards. She was trained by a nun years ago to do the interpreting. She gave me an address and I took a friend with me.

When we got to the door, "You can come in, but no one else. She must stay behind."

I have been telling the fortunes of some of the caregivers here. I take my cards and go out to the common room in my wheelchair.

Why am I not surprised that you are now taking over the nursing home? What are the caregivers' fortunes? What do you tell them? ...to be very attentive to the lovely woman in room 167 B... and if they are not...Well, I see here, it is too frightening to interpret.

Do you want me to tell your fortune, Donna?

Sure. I've always been afraid of fortune tellers. My Granny would not have approved. She believed in talking to Jesus.

It's better if you don't know anything about the person.

I will ask you to pull the cards.

You are a loving person.

You have a sister who is well off.

You will have money, but you will work for it.

You had trials when you were young.

You have a sickness, but you will have good doctors.

You are dependent on the men in your family.

You have a strong will that is dependent on your heart.

I think you are a cheat'in fortuneteller, Jule.

No one ever told me their fortune is wrong.

Can I ask you a specific question?

Sure.

Will my granddaughter pass the Nursing Board?

(*I pull the ace of diamonds.*)

That's a good one. She will ace it!

Will I finish the book I am working on?

(*I pull the jack of clubs.*)

Yes, you will, but you will need some help.

It's not good to pull the three of clubs.

Don't tell me why. That's too creepy.

I have other special powers of intuition, ESP. When I was working in Kentucky, I was headed to Churchill Downs to the horse races on the weekend. I was working for a doctor everyone called Doctor S. for Selinsky. He gave me $20.00 and told me to bet on a horse for him.

Turns out, when I got to the race, one of the horses was named Doc S. I bet on him and won $50.00 for the doctor!

My mother and I played the stock market together. One day, I looked at someone on an apple phone and I get this strong feeling all day. I should invest more in this company. Apple stayed on my mind. The next day, they came out with the Apple watch.

Another time, I saw a billboard with the word Schwab on it. I thought about the Schwab Steel Company. I invested money in that company and they sold out the next day.

Got to go. You'll have to hold court with 'otheas,' and captivate them with your Southern charm. I love you, Jule.

Oh Donna. Get me one of those big bars of dark chocolate, in the low 70s, 71, 72. Not over 72. It gets bitter. No rush. Just when you come again.

Got it. Let me guess. They have it at Walgreens???

Yes. They have the only kind I like.

A few days later

You look pretty today. Your cheeks are rosy.

My cheeks are always rosy. I'm going to physical therapy soon.

Good. I can't stay very long anyway. I'll leave when he comes. Do you get in the wheelchair and go out into the common room?

Yes, everyday.

Great.

A few days later.

Some of the Unitarians came to see me yesterday and brought those flowers. I love red roses.

Why did you join the Fairhope Unitarian Fellowship when you moved here to retire?

Their seven principles are similar to what I learned at the Jewish Synagogue.

We were reformed Jews. I went to Jewish Sunday School and had a Jewish Confirmation. I was the only little girl dressed like a bride that day for the Confirmation. Mother made me dress up because I was chosen to read by myself.

At the Unitarians, I was in the kitchen every Sunday to help prepare cookies and coffee for after the program. I asked them what I had to do to become a member and they said, "Just sign the book."

That's where we met.

Oh, that's right. Did you see me play percussion with the Back Porch Singers? I played that small tom tom drum with a mallet. All of us sang. I took piano lessons when I was a girl so I know how to read music.

There's your physical therapist. I've got to go. No food in the frig at home and clothes to wash. You look so good in that dark blue today.

This is not blue. This is periwinkle! I think you are color blind.

Really? Way down on my worry list today.

Donna, do you ever forget if a quote comes from the Bible or Shakespeare?

Got to go. Parting is such sweet sorrow.

I know that one.

Chapter 9

One Diamond Stud

One hot August evening I am traveling from Fairhope to Wichita Falls, Texas. Shortly after I leave, I hear on the radio, a tornado warning out west where I am heading. Soon the rain is so heavy my windshield wipers are thudding as fast as they can. I can't see at all when I stop under a bridge and put on my hazards. I sit for about fifteen minutes and try to decide what to do. I have gone too far to just turn back. A big truck suddenly pulls up beside me. I think he is stopping for the rain too. He rolls down his window and says "Follow me ma'am. You got a CB (radio)? My handle is 'One Diamond Stud.'"

"Yes, Miss Christmas calling One Diamond Stud 10-4." I lose track of time. There is little traffic on the road and the large yellow lights on the rear of the 18-wheeler makes for easy following. Our talk is limited to warnings about dips in the road and intersections.

At about 4 p.m. the truck driver calls, "I'm pulling into the truck stop coming up. They advertise the best breakfast in Texas."

He comes to my car and offers his hand. "Will you have breakfast with me?" He is tall and thin, a blond young man, about 19, I guess. I see a diamond pinned to his tie. Grinning, he says, "You did a good job. You were a perfect follower." *I am more than twice his age. If he notices, he doesn't show it.*

Come on, Jule. Get to the good part.

What? He escorts me into the restaurant. I thank him and say, "May I ask you how you chose your handle?"

"I dropped out of college my freshman year when my dad died. My aunt removed the diamond from her engagement ring and gave it to me for good luck. I left school to help my mother but hope to go back in a few years."

Leaving, I say, "You turned what might have been a frightening experience into a pleasurable adventure. I will always remember you and the good luck you brought me. Use the skills you learned as a truck driver and get back into school. When you leave in a truck, you have to get there on time with that load. There may be setbacks, but failure is not an option."

"I never thought about it that way."

He gets into the yellow cab of his big 18- wheeler and drives away.

"Miss Christmas calling One Diamond Stud. I appreciate your help. 10-4."

"One Diamond Stud pulling out. 10-4."

That's it? You never see him again? This is a love story, Jule. You remember him and these details after all these years. You don't jump into the big yellow cab to hug and kiss him? I would have.

Oh Donna…That would not have been propa. I was raised to be a Southern lady.

***

Did you date anyone in high school?

No, I was not interested much then. I went to the picture show with boys, but not a real date, no. However, I went through school with a boy named Richard. I thought he was interesting—smart and good looking. We never spoke. At our high school graduation, he came up to me and said, "You were always the one I loved."

That is an amazing story. Didn't you know how to flirt?

Oh, Donna.

***

I know it is about time I get married. Several of my friends are married. I meet Charles Moon in the geology department at the University of Texas. He is quiet and nice to me, rather introverted. I like his family and they like me, glad he has found a wife.

I dive into learning to cook and clean a house. You'd be surprised the way some people vacuum. They run a vacuum sideways instead of long ways so you can get in the corners.

I never thought there was a right way to vacuum. In fact, I try not to think about vacuuming at all. I will organize my vacuum notes right next to my hanger notes, Jule.

There is a right way to do everything, no matter how menial the task.

I get *The Joy of Cooking* and learn how to cook nutritious meals.

It turns out this composed husband is also passive aggressive, even mean. He never hits me or anything, but I am very unhappy. I am able to stay because he is gone so much, traveling to oil sites. He worked for Halliburton.

Oh, my daddy was a roughneck, worked in oil fields, in the derrick, for Halliburton. I have a silver cigarette lighter given to him with the company name engraved on the front.

Sure 'nough.

Very few people divorce in those days. I know I will have to go home to my parents and admit I made a big mistake. After seventeen years of marriage and no children, I remember the day I decide I will divorce.

I get pregnant. A few weeks later, I am driving along in my car when I get in severe pain. I manage to drive into my yard and jump out at the front door. When my husband comes home, I am lying in a pool of blood on the kitchen floor.

The only thing he said to me is, "Why in the hell did you pull up at the front door and make muddy ruts in the yard?"

***

My life changes for me ten years later when I meet, Bill Stephens, the love of my life. We are at a social work convention looking at books and begin to chat. He asks me if I might have dinner with him that evening. We spend the rest of our time together.

In separate rooms, Donna.

I'm sorry.

He was an interesting man: a B.A. in accounting and an M.A. in social work, with licenses in hospital administration and Criminal Social Work. Bill was also an ordained Methodist minister.

Did he go to church?

Oh, yes, and sang in the choir.

I eventually move to Kentucky with him, but we never marry. In his obituary, they name me as his wife and he includes me in his will. He was seventy-five when he died.

So young?

We had many wonderful years together. But, he worked too hard. He would not stop to rest. For example, if he worked in the yard, he would not take a break. I'd beg him to come in and get a glass of cool water. He did not take care of himself. There were some serious health problems later in life and he lost an eye.

I was left the house we owned together in Kentucky and I sold it to enable me to move back to Fairhope. I guess Bill died about thirty years ago now.

I'm sorry…But you still have men in your life, Jule---the cowboys.

Chapter 10

Do you need anything Jule?

Yes. Will you pick up a "23" calendar for me, a Border collie calendar like I had last year?

I'll see if I can find one.

Let's invite the mayor to your 104th birthday party this year. It's a big deal..

If I make it.

You always say that. Of course you'll make it. We'll have another grand party.

***

Two pet shops and no Border collie calendars,

I'll get this calendar with cute puppies on each page.

She'll like this one.

Hi, Jule. Give me some tape and I'll put your calendar up. Look at these puppies.

Oh… I wanted another Border collie calendar.

I know you did. I couldn't find one. Went to two pet stores.

Leslie Ann got one for me last year. Oh… this is ok. Tape it up. Thank you, Donna.

Border collies herd sheep, you know. Shelties herd small sheep. My first dog, Laddie, was a sheep dog. They are from the Shetland Islands, small with short legs. I asked for a Border collie at the Haven Animal Shelter in Fairhope when I moved back. I finally got the call. *We have a Border.*

At first he was afraid of me. I stood away from him holding food in   my hand, a little closer every day. Finally he came up to me.

I am a dog whisperer. I did not force him. On the third day, he ate.

One night Laddie was running up and down the fence around my house.

A man was trying to get in the window. He bit him and saved my life.

Another time after I moved to Fairhope, I heard a terrible noise at night like someone broke the door down. Laddie was going crazy. He did his job and they ran away.

I was sure he was stolen when I missed him for hours one morning. I called and called for him all day. I found him under a blanket on a chair!

Why didn't you whisper?

Oh, Donna.

Laddie lived to be sixteen. I grieved.

Open Letter to Cats by Laddie Moon

Unaccustomed as I am to addressing felines, I gladly take pen in paw to write this letter. Being myself a most amicable, effusive, docile, and dutiful breed, I hardly know how to approach those of such discerning, disarming, indifferent, and independent nature. People are fond of saying how intelligent you are, how self-possessed, not one to be taken advantage of or tricked by treats into performing nonsensical acts for the entertainment of human beings the way we canines must.

I am sure it would never occur to you to allow yourself to be in a harness and led about on a leash. You probably don't even consider yourself spoiled, having your own private bathroom, personal chair, or preferred lap. I, on the other hand, dare not sit on the sofa. Moreover, something in the deep recesses of my puppyhood memories causes me to eschew beds, lest some terrible, unknown fate befall me.

Of course, I am provided with living quarters, albeit of rough-hewn pine, outside in the back yard which domicile in people's vernacular equates with being kicked out of the house. Sometimes my mistress even lets me come into the house, not I suspect, because it is a necessary advantage to me, but because it makes her feel better.

Your legendary beauty and private self has earned you the right to a life of languid luxury, whilst we dogs are forced to work for a living—walking our masters to ease their arthritic pain and lose fat, guiding, guarding, fetching, hunting, herding, rescuing, etc. Then, after spending grueling hours at training camps, whose motto can be read over their formidable iron gate, OBEDIENCE FOREVER, we must then struggle to pass tests or "graduate," i,e, be set free to leave.

A point about your classic looks. Every one of you looks like—well—a cat. Same pointy ears, cute little nose, cupid's bow lips, and sexy body. Furry or plain, short-tailed or long, you are beautiful. Some dogs are pretty, okay, but on the whole, most look like a skeleton, a scarecrow, a witch riding a broomstick in a hurricane, or a rag mop. I must admit people often remark that I am good-looking but then I never know if they mean it or just like the way I work overtime at being friendly in order to get a compliment.

People are known to adopt you at the drop of a hat, or should I say, cat. All you must do is show up, sidle sinuously alongside a human leg, utter your classic two-tone seductive "meow," and *voila*--you're in. Such behavior on our part, I can tell you, accompanied by our particular vocal, barking, would garner an immediate phone call to the dog catcher.

Something else hard for us dogs to comprehend—I'm told people are known to adopt more than one of you at a time. I recently met a person who adopted twelve. I and my mistress—she likes to think of herself as my "Mama"—met this lady on one of our daily walks. She as much as said she could never turn any one of you away, no matter what.

In my own experience, I was abandoned twice, walked the streets of New Orleans near starvation, then was taken home for a short time, then given up again and deposited at a shelter---you know, the euphemism for dog pound—where I was adopted by my Fairhope mistress. In order to avoid the appearance of ingratitude and a third such horror in my life, I have to roll over on my back at the sight of her, wag my tail incessantly, fling back my ears, make goo goo eyes with my big browns, and "come," whether I like it or not.   Jule Moon

**

Sorry, Jule. I couldn't get back last week. How are you?

Oh, where is the calendar I put on your closet door? That's not the calendar I bought.

Leslie Ann found a Border collie calendar.

Where did she find it?

I think she went to Foley.

Oh…Oh…I'm glad you're happy.

He wants to declare war!

Who's going to declare war?

You know who I'm talking about, the crazy man, if he gets elected again.

Jane, a friend of mine, tells her husband when he starts raving about politics, "What can you do about that today? If there is nothing, then let it go. Have some avocado toast. Donna is visiting."

Would you rather be right or be happy, Jule? I already know the answer to that question.

***

Today is my son's 43rd birthday. He's an English teacher like I was, but he lives in Amsterdam. I should have looked at my choices when I was young. Doesn't that sound like fun? I just put my head down and got to work because I knew I had to pay the bills. I loved teaching like he does.

He teaches English to Dutch businessmen and government officials, men and women. In The Netherlands, the government pays for a year of Dutch lessons in the evenings. If you go to 80% of the classes and pass a test on reading, writing, and speaking Dutch---only then— can you apply for a residency visa to live and work there. He has been living there twelve years.

What company?

He's on his own.

Free lancing.

Yes, I guess that's what you could call it. He goes beneath the surface to find out what the student needs to learn. It's more complex than teaching English to a native speaker. Even though the Dutch take English in school, there are nuances they are expected to pick up on in certain situations. The ability to move into a management position may be based on their understanding of colloquialisms in English; how smoothly they handle the global economy questions or a lawsuit, for example.

I enjoy listening when Benjamin explains, "the bottom line" or "Don't get into the weeds." He goes into offices when employees are given a day to study English in groups. He also does local theater and I'm sure uses his body language to teach.

That's what a good teacher does. Finds out what the student needs to know.

I love Amsterdam, but I had to ask Benjamin why he moved as far away from his poor ole mama as he could. I thought at first that he would "scratch that itch" and come back. Then one day, he said, "Mama, I'm not ever coming back to the states to live." I cried.

He went to Nepal for a summer to help teachers learn how to teach English. He's is a giving person. I framed a picture of him with the Nepal teachers and their students after they put a robe on him and a stole around his neck.

Traveling has been fun and interesting following Benjamin around Europe, Japan, Prague…Want to hear a narrative poem I wrote?

Sure.

Body Memory

In Prague, a crowd of working people with their lunch pails, rush from every direction, past the statue of Dvorak and into the Rudolfinum Concert Hall.

We are there to hear Emanuel Ax, pianist.

Seated in the balcony high above the piano, I see the entire

keyboard, a perfect view in the 1885 Concert Hall in Neo Renaissance style.

The musician begins touching the keys gently, ever so gently,

to invite us into his listening conversation from Beethoven's

Concerto, number 4.

Every finger dances over the black and white keys reflecting

his love and passion for the piece, then a pause, a racing

and pounding staccato.

False emotions cannot linger as the notes from the left and

from the right circle in a magic blend.

My ears receive the sound as pure pleasure.

No moment is more important than the next.

Humility and respect waft from the instrument to the listeners.

The piano, pianist, and audience begin to breathe as one.

Why does a writer use words to describe an unforgettable music

experience?

It is a mystery.

Many years later when I hear a piano, I listen from my right,

from my left. I do not think I will ever feel that sound again.

dfo

***

Kurt called and said they have a place in the nursing home for me. He says I can't afford this around the clock care. I understand.

Ken, in my writing group, said he will take Buddy. He has two other dogs and Buddy has been over there before. Says he'll bring him to visit me every week.

You sound like you are taking your own advice: Happiness in life depends upon one's ability to adapt.

How will I get over there? I can't walk.

In an ambulance. It will be here in the morning about 10 o'clock.

Good. I'll have time to put on my make-up.

The Next Morning

I have to take a picture of you lying with your back propped up on that bed, Jule. I love the huge sunglasses. You look like Audrey Hepburn. *Only Jule could look elegant on a gurney going to a nursing home.*

Don't drop me now!

They won't, Jule, you only weigh ninety- seven pounds.

Get my house shoes, Donna.

Oh, you handed me two left shoes! I can't put these on.

Put them on, Jule. They look like socks! It will be okay. That's what they handed me.

I can't go with two left shoes!

Look, I can slip them on. They look alike. See?

People don't pay attention to what they are doing. Who handed you two left shoes?

Jule, it doesn't matter. The guys have to leave.

Smile for the camera.

I will ride behind the ambulance and see that you get settled.

Two left shoes. Ugh.

Queen of Know

I've grown accustomed to my face
Every day a new surprise
Eyelashes left without a trace
My eyebrows faint about my eyes

Each day my blue eyes pale to powder gray
I get thinner all the while
My dimples swallowed by a fold
Dull lips define a smile can fill

A fatalist all my life
I ponder feet the cells and magnetic plates
Accept what is offered here
I've grown accustomed to my fate

Jule Moon

Chapter 10

Nursing Home

How are you?

Green beans out of a can, twenty-six days in a row

It would probably help if you didn't count.

Poem: Green Beans Saga

My apologies to Joyce Kilmer who wrote: "I think that I shall never see a poem as lovely as a tree."

I think that I shall never see

Any food but green beans served to me

Is that the only veggies that they buy

After twenty-six days of them, I cry?

The food I ate where I had been

I did not have to pretend was medicine

Poems are made by fools like me

Instead of green beans, I would rather eat a tree.

Frustration: Definition according to me:

Someone being faced with an intolerable situation and is being stymied.

I didn't look it up in Webster, but trust me on this.

I live in an institution where meals, methodologically and without feeling, are served blind to their destination. I count twenty-six days out of thirty, canned green beans, tasteless and mushy. I get one serving on my plate and two bowls of green beans on the side!

Now to the subject of frustration: When I see the beans I want to throw them on the floor (visualize this). I have seen enough of this type of preposterous behavior to know it's not out of the question because there is no question about it—I want to throw the beans.

So, when I see them and nothing else, I pretend they are medicine. I formerly I looked forward to lunch. Now I face it with dread, as if I were a Roman Centurion facing a lion. It's just that scary.

So daily I say a little prayer that the Creator will send forth something else.

My mother lived to be 101. I thought I would die that year. Now I am going to have a big party at 104!

If I make it.

Remember what we agreed not to talk about?

Sometimes I see fish, chicken or pork chops on your tray. I'll bring you some fresh vegetables when I cook them. They did get your gluten-free bread.

Your hair looks nice today.

We go to the beauty shop on Wednesday. She does same, same, same for everyone. She rolls it under. I want my bangs rolled down and all the others up to my face. I brush it out. Whatever it is, I am difficult. I know I'm a pain to these people.

I dream of somewhere to be

Where someone cares about me

And I and everyone can be free!

I'm into self-pity.

That's okay, I think I understand why you're sad.

I learn something about you every time we're together.

I can't even pout very long about the Border collie calendar.

A month later after my vacation

Jule's mouth is hanging open and it always scares me. But she immediately looks up with a big smile.

You're back!

When I return I find her handwritten note in the mail.

"Have I told you recently that I love you?"

That's Jule. Her mantra is: Life for me is all about people.

(*After she opens the package wrapped in "Miffy bunny" paper from Amsterdam*)

I love this brown and orange throw. Is it cotton?

I notice that Vivian (her roommate) always has a colorful throw or quilt on her bed. **"I want you to have something to look at."**

Oh, not on the bed. This is too pretty.

Yes, on the bed. I want you to have something pleasing on your bed.

Is it cotton? It feels so good.

I don't know.

Something strange happened last night. I was writing a poem and I heard music across the room to go with it. The music was right up there on the wall.

You told me you can think about some piece of music and you can play it in your head and enjoy it. Or you can play the piano in your mind and visualize the keys. That's extraordinary.

I'm not free! (tears in her eyes) I'm not free here. I have to do what they tell me! When I tell them to do something, they don't do it. Nobody knows how to follow directions. My closet should be arranged beginning with my gowns, then my bed jackets, my tops, my skirts then my sweaters. Nobody hangs anything up and when they do, my clothes are put anywhere! You know when I ask somebody to find something, they grab a few hangers, and they never find what I am looking for! You are supposed to…

I know. I have had the Jule Moon hanger lesson s*everal times*.

They obviously have not had their lesson.

Have you ever heard "Choose your battles." or "How important is it?"

Yes, Yes, I know all that. I am a psychologist!

Okay. Do you want this throw I brought you on your bed? You don't do you? You've kicked it down to the end… *It's not all cotton. She never uses it.*

***

Your bedside drawer needs cleaning. It is so stuffed, you can't find anything. Let's take everything out and put some of this stuff elsewhere. It is yucky with something wet in the bottom.

I have to be able to find things!

She goes through the whole drawer and doesn't discard a single item.

Since everything is out, I'll give it a good cleaning.

Ode to Donna

Nothing too menial for her

Goes to a task like a professional

House cleaner or chimney sweep

Offer her a treasure to give

Hankie, for example

Modestly denies, too pristine, nothing to clean

Also: reimbursement for shopping

Maybe a secret billionaire

Managed to force a plant for her garden

Bingo, natural acceptance

When it comes to ivy

With dirt!

***

I cannot help to contemplate and compare: Jule Moon began life, bedridden, writing poetry at six years old. Now at 104, her body fails her again but she remains— the persistent poet.

Got to go. *I bend to kiss her on the cheek.*

Don't touch my hair!

Donna Orchard

Bye Jule. I love you.

Wisdom by Jule Moon

1. Don't Be a Sheep.
2. Do you want to be happy? Learn to adapt.
3. Think About What you are Doing.
4. Organize your life.
5. Have a sense of purpose.
6. Take a Stand.
7. Honor your family.
8. Nurture life-time friends.
9. Accept what you can't change.
10. Establish a Routine.
11. Get your education. You'll need it.
12. Write what you know.
13. Be a joiner.
14. Watch what you eat. Food is important.
15. Have color in your life.
16. Be Thankful.
17. Science pervades everything.
18. Be habitual and predictable.
19. Dogs
20. Southern Lady

21. spiritual
22. Intuition and science coincide
23. Business woman
24. Importance of Place
25. You think you do everything yourself? Oh, No!
26. Self-confident
27. Identify needs. Organize a plan to meet them.
28. Curiosity
29. Bible or Shakespeare ?
30. What happens when your body gives up before your mind?

Sherds

a Memoir

by

Jule Moon

2006

"Hi Jule."

"Here, I signed one of my books for you.

"Sherds a Memoir. I have to admit that I don't understand the title. What is a 'sherd'?"

"Sherds are clay pieces left behind from the indigenous people, the American Indians. The Southwestern Indians initially settled as farmers. Then some began making clay pots.

At the University of Texas, Native Americans became a life-long interest.

I majored in geology and moved from the intuitive to the scientific.

I'm Riding Out the Virus

I'm riding out the virus with my dog

My lone companion, giving joy and comfort

This reminds me of the ride of the Depression, WWII, 9/11 and hurricanes.

Donna Orchard

I will get out my mending long neglected
And glue in the rhinestone fallen out in 2018
That stack of books set out on the dining table
Will rest at last on the bookshelf as is proper.

And every day I'll have my care giver take
My guardian angel, Buddy for his walk.
I'll cut two inches off my vintage nightgowns
Which are long because I've shrunk two inches.

How innumerable are the advantages of quarantine!
I know that someday when all this is over
And I'll survive to see the next one
I'll be accomplished, neat and organized
The one remaining challenge I can't conquer
Is you, Dear Friend, await.

Jule Moon

All the World's a Doctor's Office
Inspired by a poem by William Shakespeare
By Jule Moon

All the World's a doctor's office
All the men and women merely patients
And one man in his time loses many parts
First the thirty-year-old with carpal
Tunnel from too much laptop tapping
And smart phone punching
Then the forty-year-old with sprained ankles
From too much freestyle and line dancing
Then the fifty-year-old with house maid's
Knees and aching heels from five-inch stilts
And then the sixty-year-old with baggy
Eyes and drugstore readers
Followed by the seventy-year-old with
Lumbar pains from too much
Sitting and rotator cuff separation from
Stretching in Tai Chi
Then the eighty-year-old
With trembling hands and hesitant
Feet in tennis shoes
The ninety-year old with

Snow white hair and disappearing neck

And finally the hundred-year-old

With nothing left to lose.

Narrative Poem

The Word I Could Not Say in a Letter to my Friends

When I was eleven-years-old I heard the neighbor boy say "shit." When I learned what it meant, I was shocked by him and all such others afterward.

All my life I heard it and since I lived in the South, I figured it was a Southern thing. You know we have so many sayings like, y'all and ain't. But as a Southern girl born in Georgia and later moved to Alabama, I have earned three degrees at the University of Texas.

By the Grace of Joshua (I prefer the original) here I am now. I can feel good when it is easier to feel bad.

Portrait of a Caregiver

Don't call the FBI, call Sarah. She handles dozens of intersects daily. When I need an item, I ask her to search. I call Sarah when I am missing something—anything. My loud voice evokes a major tragedy. I am bedridden and someone has moved a 'thing.' It does not matter if it is a pair of scissors or the heart pill that keeps me alive.

Sarah knows she does not mean 'look.' Jule means 'search.' It will not be easy. She does not ask anyone else, 'Sarah.'

No one ever listens. Pay attention! That's what my mother taught me. They do not pay attention. Nobody who packs me pays attention. The Japanese prints are not sold together! Where is the jeweled gray top I wore at my 100th birthday party? The tears fall. I have lost everything.

I call from the bed if Sarah is in the kitchen. Call her when she is in the bathroom. Call her at home with her husband and children. Call when she is finally taking a break from a 12-hour shift. Sarah always answers. It is Jule—a bond over our admiration and dislike for each other. "Sarah is a child!" I roll my eyes.

She knows I am persnickety. She is suited for the job and fulfills the requirements, insistent on finishing every task before the night caregiver comes. She doesn't cook for her family, but she cooks for me. She walks in from stirring the ground meat for chili. At dinner I complain that is too hot.

Going to the store is an event when I cannot move out of this bed. I like garnishments on my food. Where is the salsa, more butter? This broccoli has no taste! More tears.

I correct everyone. I am able to come up with the exact word for what Sarah is trying to say. She thinks she should go in for an Alzheimer's test when a 102- year old has such a perfect memory. Sarah's revenge? I would rather be right than be happy.

Jule Moon

Jule Moon
by Suzanne Hudson and Joe Formichella

What a great lady, Jule Moon. Her name is certainly a name befitting an author, lyrical, like the seed for a poem. It's a name that coaxes symbolic layers from its strand of letters. It's a name that speaks a sparking existence.

Jule—a jewel, which, after an exhilarating life of learned lessons—

some harsh but ultimately uplifting—is a woman revealed in a multifaceted spark that is her smile. Even as she approaches a century's worth of living, that smile of hers is as youthful as it ever was.

Moon—a life force, a mover—of tides, of rhythms, of spirits. She is a constant and eager consumer of ideas, thoughts; ways of looking at the world that make her a magnet for good, intelligent people who are drawn to her shimmering, enviable energy. It is a thing she surely must have felt early but could not identify, as young girl welcoming to everyone and everything, unafraid where others feared to veer from the mundane, the feebly anemic status quo. Surely, she somehow already knew that listening and laughter bind us all in every way. And now, here, fortunately, she is allowing us to listen and laugh along with her.

Within these pages she shares her memories of growing up in Mobile, Alabama; her steadfast affinity to family; her unique experiences as a "career woman (and a serial one at that, growing through several professional incarnations) before that was so fashionable for a "proper lady" in the South; her loves and her losses and her strength of spirit that is so inspiring to those of us who hunger for such nourishment in our own existences.

And she is offering it to us. She has collected up the sherds of her experience and fixed them together into these reminiscences, stories, and poems for the rest of us to enjoy, And while we're at it, if we keep our hearts open, at the ready, we might just catch some of the spiritual glitter that is the soul of, yes, a truly, truly great lady.

Author Note

I have spent the last couple of years recording conversations with this most remarkable woman. In many places they are a little rough, and there are a few repeats of her life's stories, but I am keeping them in to show context in the different interviews.

I hope through them you are able to glean a little of the wit and wisdom of this marvelous woman.

Additional Books by the Author

Roughneck Daddy
Roughneck: A Daughter's Story
Behind the Schoolhouse Door

and a Children's Book:
Nanner for Nana

Made in the USA
Columbia, SC
28 June 2024

3182bd33-6811-428a-ae7a-de16e954de21R01